WILD ANIMALS
IN CROSS STITCH

WILD ANIMALS
IN CROSS STITCH

JULIE HASLER

CASSELL

ACKNOWLEDGEMENTS

I would like to give my thanks to all the people who have contributed a lot of time and effort in helping me with this book: Paul Human for the original paintings from which these designs have been produced; Steve Matthews for his help with the word-processing; Sue Dickinson, Allison Mortley, Barbara Hodgkinson, Jenny Whitlock, Stella Baddeley, Odette Robinson, Angela Clare Ferguson, Libby Shaw, Joyce Formby and Diana Hewitt for sewing up the embroideries; H. W. Peel & Co., Middlesex, for the graph paper; and Cara Ackerman, from DMC Creative World Ltd, for the fabrics and silks.

A CASSELL BOOK

First published in the UK 1993
by Cassell
Villiers House
41/47 Strand
London WC2N 5JE

Distributed in the United States
by Sterling Publishing Co., Inc.
387 Park Avenue South, New York, NY 10016-8810

Distributed in Australia
by Capricorn Link (Australia) Pty Ltd
P.O. Box 665, Lane Cove, NSW 2066

British Library Cataloguing-in-Publication Data
A catalogue record for this book is available from
the British Library

ISBN 0-304-34171-1 (hardback)
ISBN 0-304-34173-8 (paperback)

Typeset by MS Filmsetting Ltd, Frome, Somerset
Printed and bound in Hong Kong

Contents

◆

THE DESIGNS

This book is dedicated to
Yvonne and Sonny
for their love and support
over the past years

Preface

———◆———

With each passing year, the future of the world's animals becomes more uncertain. Nearly 800,000 elephants were slaughtered by poachers during the 1980s for the ivory trade, and every day up to 50 animal species face extinction. I would hope that, when we teach the alphabet to the next generation, 'E' is still for 'elephant' and not 'extinct'. Donating money to various charities is a positive step, but we can all help in our own way by not buying, and encouraging others not to buy, wildlife products such as ivory, animal skin coats and coral; and exotic pets such as monkeys, snakes, lizards and exotic birds. The long-term answer lies in changing people's attitudes and making awareness of conservation a natural part of daily life.

Sewing up these beautiful wild animal designs and displaying them in your home can be your way of showing interest in and concern for wild animals throughout the world.

Introduction

◆

The favourite stitch of our great-grandmothers, cross stitch, is becoming increasingly popular in these modern times for the decoration of household furnishings, linen, children's clothes, in fact anything which lends itself to this type of embroidery. The possibilities are endless.

Cross stitch is one of the simplest, most versatile and elegant needlecrafts, and examples of its use can be found in many different countries and different eras.

The projects in this book make beautiful gifts for family and friends: gifts with a personal touch which have taken time and care to create, which will still be treasured long after shop-bought items have been forgotten.

Whether you are an experienced or inexperienced needleworker, you will be able to find projects in this book to suit your abilities. The designs can be worked by following the charts exactly or, with imagination, you can use alternative colours to create embroideries which are uniquely yours.

You will have to bear in mind that in counted thread work, the finished piece of work will not be the same size as the charted design unless the fabric you are working on has the same number of threads per inch as the chart has squares per inch.

General Guidance

———◆———

The designs in this book are created for counted cross stitch, a very enjoyable craft which you will find easy to learn—and inexpensive too!

The fabric you sew your designs on and the number of strands of silk you use is your choice. You will find that the fabric is available in varying thread counts, and that there is a very wide range of colours: white, ecru, pink, blue, lemon and pale green, to name but a few.

I chose 14-count Aida in various colours to sew the designs in this book, using three strands of embroidery cotton for the cross stitch. Another fabric commonly used is 18-count Fine Aida, with two strands of embroidery cotton for the cross stitch. Use your imagination to choose a fabric colour that will enhance your embroidery.

The charts are easy to read. Each square on the chart represents one stitch to be taken on the fabric and each different symbol represents a different colour, the empty squares being background fabric. A colour key is given with each design.

If you wish to decorate clothing with any of the designs in this book, the most satisfactory method is to work the design over cross stitch fabric basted to the clothing material and remove the cross stitch fabric afterwards, thread by thread. This will leave behind the embroidery on the clothing material beneath.

Relax, enjoy sewing the designs, and make something beautiful for you and your home.

Cross Stitch Techniques

To begin: bring the thread through at the lower right-hand side, leaving a short length of thread on the underside of the work and anchoring it with the first few stitches as in Figures 1 and 2. Insert the needle across the mesh into the next hole above and diagonally to the left and bring it out through the hole across the mesh but immediately below. Half the stitch is now completed.

Continue in the same way to the end of the row. Your stitches should be diagonal on the right side of the fabric and vertical on the wrong side. Complete the upper half of the stitch by returning in the opposite direction, as shown in Figure 3.

Cross stitch can be worked in either direction, from right to left or left to right, but it is of the utmost importance that the upper half of each cross should lie in the same direction.

You may find it easier to sew all the black outlines first, and then fill in the colours afterwards. Choose a working method that is comfortable for you.

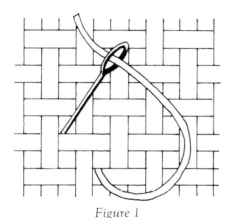

Figure 1

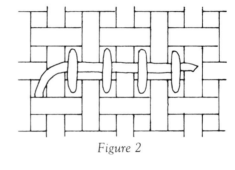

Figure 2

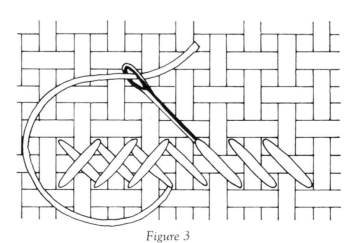

Figure 3

Materials

◆

Needles

A small blunt tapestry needle, no. 24 or 26, is best for cross stitch.

Scissors

A sharp pair of embroidery scissors is essential, especially if a mistake has to be unpicked.

Embroidery Hoop

A round plastic or wooden hoop with a screw-type tension adjuster, 4, 5 or 6 in (10, 13 or 15 cm) in diameter, is ideal for cross stitch. Place the area of fabric to be embroidered over the inner ring and gently push the outer ring over it, ensuring that the fabric is taut and the mesh straight, and gradually tighten the screw adjuster as you go.

Threads

DMC six-strand embroidery cotton has been used to colour-code the designs in this book. The number of strands used will depend on the fabric you decide to work on. Specific quantities of thread have not been stated for each design, as these will differ depending on the fabric used and the tension of the stitches.

Fabric

Do not choose a fabric which does not have an even weave, as this will distort the embroidery either vertically or horizontally. An evenweave fabric on which it is easy to count the threads should be used. There is a variety on the market in varying thread counts and colours. The most popular fabrics are Aida cloth and Hardanger cloth.

Cotton Aida is available in the following sizes: 8, 11, 14 and 18 threads per inch, which is known as Fine Aida.

Linen is available in the following sizes: 19/20, 25/26 and 30/31 threads per inch.

Hardanger is 22 threads per inch.

Preparing to Work

◆

To determine the size of the finished embroidery, count the squares on the chart for the entire width and depth of the design, and divide each by the number of threads per inch in the fabric you intend to use. This will give the dimensions in inches. Cut the fabric at least 2 in (5 cm) wider each way than the finished size to allow for finishing. To prevent the fabric from fraying, either machine-stitch or whip-stitch the outer edges or alternatively bind them with masking tape.

Find the centre of the fabric by folding it in half vertically and then horizontally. Mark the centre with a line of basting stitches both lengthwise and widthwise. To locate the centre of a design, count half the squares up the side and half the squares along the top. Where these two points meet in the middle of the design is its centre.

It is preferable to begin cross stitch at the top of the design. To find the top, count the squares up from the centre of the chart and then the number of holes up from the centre of the fabric. Ensure that the fabric is held tautly in the embroidery hoop, as this makes stitching easier, enabling the needle to be pushed through the holes without piercing the fibres of the fabric. If the fabric loosens while you work, retighten as necessary. When working, you will find it easier to have the screw in the ten o'clock position to prevent your thread from becoming tangled in the screw with each stitch. If you are left-handed, have the screw in the one o'clock position.

When working with stranded cotton, always separate the strands before threading the needle. This will give better coverage of the fabric. The number of strands will depend on the fabric count that you use.

Useful Tips

———◆———

1 When you are stitching, it is important not to pull the fabric out of shape. You can accomplish this by working the stitches in two motions, straight up through a hole in the fabric and then straight down, ensuring that the fabric remains taut. Make sure that you don't pull the thread tight—snug, but not tight. If you use this method, you will find that the thread will lie just where you want it to and not pull your fabric out of shape.

2 If your thread becomes twisted while you work, drop the needle and let it hang down freely. It will then untwist itself. Do not continue working with twisted thread as it will appear thinner and will not cover your fabric as well.

3 Never leave your needle in the design area of your work when not in use. No matter how good the needle might be, it could rust in time and mark your work permanently.

4 Do not carry thread across the back of an open expanse of fabric. If you are working separate areas of the same colour, fasten off the thread and begin again. Loose threads, especially dark colours, will be visible from the right side of your work when the project is completed.

Finishing

———◆———

When the embroidery is finished, it will need to be pressed. Place the finished work right side down on your ironing board, cover it with a thin, slightly dampened cloth, and iron.

If you intend to frame the finished embroidery yourself, you will need to block it. Cut a piece of board to the desired size and place the finished em-broidery over it. Fold the surplus fabric to the back and secure along the top edge of the board with pins. Pull firmly over the opposite edge and pin in position.

Repeat this procedure along both side edges, pulling the fabric until it is lying taut on the board.

Secure at the back by lacing from side to side on all four sides with strong thread. Remove the pins. Your embroidery is now ready to be framed. The best result will be achieved if you take it to a professional framer. If you are having a glazed frame, the effect will be improved by using non-reflective glass. Although it is slightly more expensive, it is well worth it.

After-care of Your Cross Stitch Embroideries

———◆———

You may find at some stage that your cross stitch projects will need to be laundered. This is no problem: just follow the simple advice supplied by DMC in conjunction with their six-stranded cotton. The following recommendations are for washing embroidery separately from all other laundry.

	COTTON OR LINEN FABRIC	SYNTHETIC FABRIC
RECOMMENDED WASHING	Wash in warm, soapy water. Rinse thoroughly. Squeeze without twisting and hang to dry. Iron on reverse side using two layers of white linen.	Not recommended.
BLEACHING OR WHITENING AGENT	Product should be diluted according to manufacturer's instructions. The embroidery should be pre-soaked in clean water first, then soaked for five minutes in a solution of about 1 tablespoon of bleaching agent per quart (1.1 l) of cold water. Rinse thoroughly in cold water.	The same instructions are recommended if the white of the fabric is not of a high standard. If the fabric is a pure white (white with a bluish tinge) do not use bleaching or whitening agent.
DRY CLEANING	Avoid dry cleaning. Some spot removers (benzine, trichlorethylene) can be used for an occasional small stain.	Not recommended, even for occasional small stains.

Fox

—◆—

There are about a dozen species of fox, all approximately the same size and all members of the dog family. Their main prey is small mammals such as rabbits and mice, but they also eat birds, small insects, earthworms and fruit.

The familiar red fox is very successful despite its persecution by man. It is found all over Europe, North Africa, much of Asia down to central India and Vietnam, and in North America. Not only has it survived hunting, but the species has been spread more widely by it, as foxes were introduced to Australia and parts of America to provide huntsmen with something to chase.

The fox is a solitary animal, living in the brushland or along the forest edges. Hunting is a solitary activity, and foxes do not join forces to attack large animals. Unlike dogs, foxes are mainly nocturnal in their habits, finding hidden food by sniffing it out. They rarely hunt by day, but will do so if they are pressed to find food to feed a litter of young.

There are usually four young in a litter, raised in burrows which the foxes dig. The male fox (the dog) usually stays with its mate (the vixen) and assists in feeding and rearing the young.

■	310 black	◪	758 pale brick red
▥	702 Kelly green	z	726 light topaz yellow
⫶	704 bright chartreuse green	c	414 steel grey
◉	632 chocolate brown	＝	3013 light khaki green
·	white	x	869 hazelnut brown
v	920 medium copper	∧	3011 dark khaki green
‹	367 dark pistachio green	o	3328 medium salmon red

Chipmunk

———◆———

The chipmunk is a small, striped, brightly coloured member of the squirrel family found throughout most of North America. There are many varieties of chipmunk, all feeding on nuts or seeds, but occasionally making a meal of insects, mushrooms or birds' eggs. The chipmunk stuffs its cheek-pouches with food and then carries it to a safe place to eat or store it. Some chipmunks hibernate during periods of extreme cold.

Photo on p. 20

■	310 black	◣	3024 very light brown grey
⊙	3031 very dark brown	⊂	611 dark drab brown
⋅	676 light old gold	⊠	610 very dark drab brown
⊠	729 medium old gold	⊽	612 drab brown
⧄	989 light forest green	⊟	356 medium brick red
‖	3363 loden green	⨍	436 tan brown
⊡	3348 light yellow green	⊞	977 golden brown
⊡	white		

CHIPMUNK
See pp. 18–19

· 20 ·

GAZELLE
See pp. 22–3

Gazelle

———◆———

The gazelle is a small graceful antelope with S-shaped horns. It lives in herds on the open grasslands of Africa and Asia in groups of up to 30, and is common around water-holes. The two-tone coloration of the gazelle acts as countershading to hide it from its predators. Its diet consists mainly of grass, herbs and woody plants, depending on their availability, but it will generally eat whatever is greenest.

In the breeding season, the male will establish a territory which will actively exclude other mature males. The gazelle breeds seasonally so that the birth of the young coincides with the vegetation flush in early spring or early rains. The female will go off on her own to give birth, and the fawn will lie out for the first few weeks of its life, joining the group when it can run sufficiently well.

Many species of gazelle have been greatly reduced by man.

Photo on p. 21

■	310 black	○	839 dark beige brown
✗	645 dark beaver grey	⫿	319 very dark pistachio green
⊙	317 medium steel grey	⸬	703 chartreuse green
•	white	©	911 medium emerald green
⋁	422 light tan beige	⋀	3051 dark grey green

Lion Cub

The lion is the only social cat. It lives in prides of several lionesses and their cubs and one or two adult male lions. The lioness will usually spend her life in her original pride but the young male lions will leave the mother's pride and join another. The lion's roar is a means of keeping in touch with other members of the pride. The male lion is lazy and inactive much of the time, leaving the lionesses to do most of the hunting, but claiming first share of the kill. The lion's main prey is large animals such as zebras, buffaloes and antelopes. It will lie in wait, usually near a water-hole, then, when its prey gets close, rush at it, striking with its large paws and usually breaking the animal's neck.

The lion lives in the open grassy plains and bush country of Africa and Asia, where it is exposed to the sun. Its fur is short and coarse, unlike the soft fur of other cats, which has the advantage of making it less attractive to the fur hunter. The male lion has a bushy mane which makes it hard for it to conceal itself. A large male can weigh up to 500 lb (226 kg). The female is smaller, weighing up to 300 lb (136 kg), and has no mane. The newly born lion cubs have lightly spotted coats, but these spots disappear when they are about six months old.

Lions were once common in south-west Asia and the lands around the eastern Mediterranean. However, in this area they have now been hunted almost to extinction. Outside of Africa they occur only in the Gir forest of north-west India where a small number survive under government protection.

■	310 black	‖	841 light beige brown
⁛	677 very light old gold	V	739 fawn beige
T	3364 light loden green	C	738 very light tan
●	317 medium steel grey	⧄	3348 light yellow green
☒	647 medium beaver grey	∧	912 light emerald green
⊡	white		

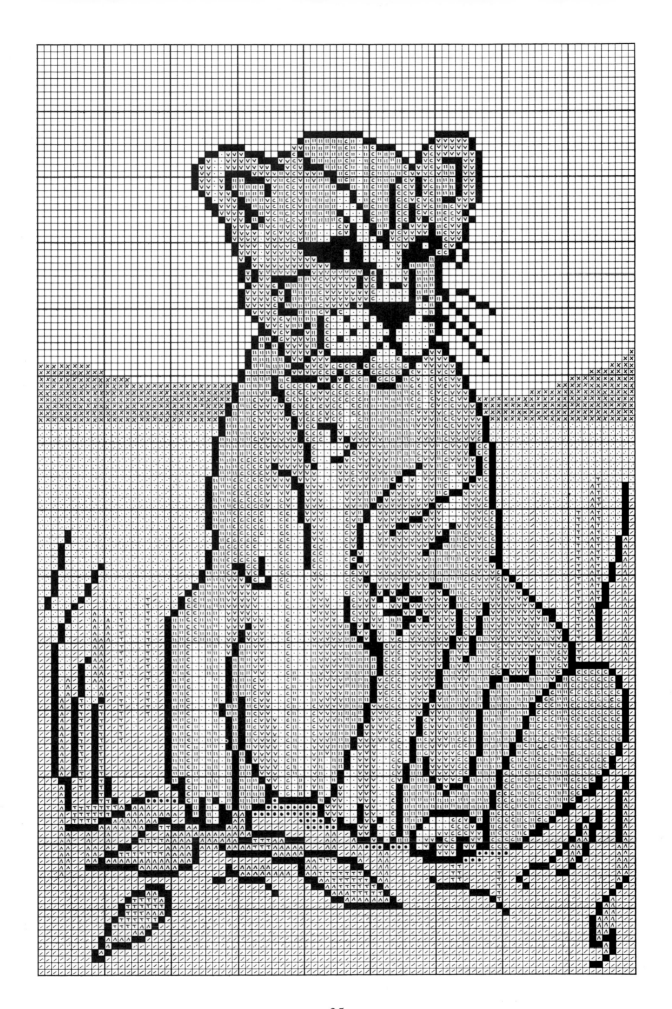

Indian Elephant

The Indian elephant is found from India eastward to Indo-China and south into Sumatra. It is smaller in overall size, and has relatively small ears by comparison to the African elephant. Bull elephants measure just under 9 ft (2.7 m) in height at the shoulders, and average $3\frac{1}{2}$ tons in weight. The tusks of the elephant are actually huge upper incisor teeth. The tusks grow only 4 in (10 cm) a year, and because they often break, are rarely more than 8 ft (2.4 m) long. The unique feature of the elephant is its trunk, an elongated nose which allows the animal to eat and drink without having to kneel. It also uses its trunk to pluck leaves and creepers from high above its head in the forests. To drink, it sucks water up into the trunk and squirts it into its mouth. Also, to keep its skin in good condition, it squirts water over its back from its trunk.

Because of the inefficiency of the elephant's digestive system (only about 40 per cent of the food eaten is digested), it consumes masses of leaves, twigs and bark stripped from trees. It consumes up to 220 lb (100 kg) of food each day. The elephant can be very destructive, as it will push over a tree to get to the highest growth.

Unfortunately, the elephant population has been greatly diminished as a result of hunting for the ivory trade.

Photo on p. 28

■	310 black	∧	869 hazelnut brown
●	645 dark beaver grey	C	3363 loden green
·	white	O	367 dark pistachio green
‖	612 drab brown	7	727 very light topaz yellow
V	932 light antique blue	╱	648 light beaver grey
✕	3348 light yellow green	∴	646 beaver grey

INDIAN ELEPHANT
See pp. 26–7

CHIMPANZEE
See pp. 30–1

Chimpanzee

◆

The chimpanzee is part of the ape family, native to the forests of tropical Africa. An adult male can weigh almost 150 lb (68 kg) and grow up to 5 ft (1.5 m) tall. The female is slightly smaller. The chimpanzee's body is more sparsely haired than many other species of the ape family. It is principally vegetarian, feeding on fruits, nuts and leaves, although when kept in captivity it quickly learns to eat similar foods to man. It is a tree-dwelling primate, building its nest in branches several feet above the forest floor.

The chimpanzee uses its long arms and large feet to climb about in the trees. It is quite able to walk erect, but usually moves about on all fours, using the knuckles of its hands and its flat hind-feet for support. It travels in loosely organized groups using its own simple 'language' of sounds.

The chimpanzee's intelligence and similarity to man has unfortunately led to its decline in population. Not only are chimpanzees experimented on in the study of behaviour and disease, but their ability to learn tricks and master skills which require a degree of reasoning has led to an illegal trade to supply young animals. Older animals in captivity often become unpredictable and are destroyed.

Photo on p. 29

■	310 black	☒	437 light tan brown
▥	413 very dark steel grey	◉	610 very dark drab brown
⋅	945 light apricot	⊻	3013 light khaki green
▪	white	Ⓒ	3051 dark grey green
▨	471 light avocado green		

Seal

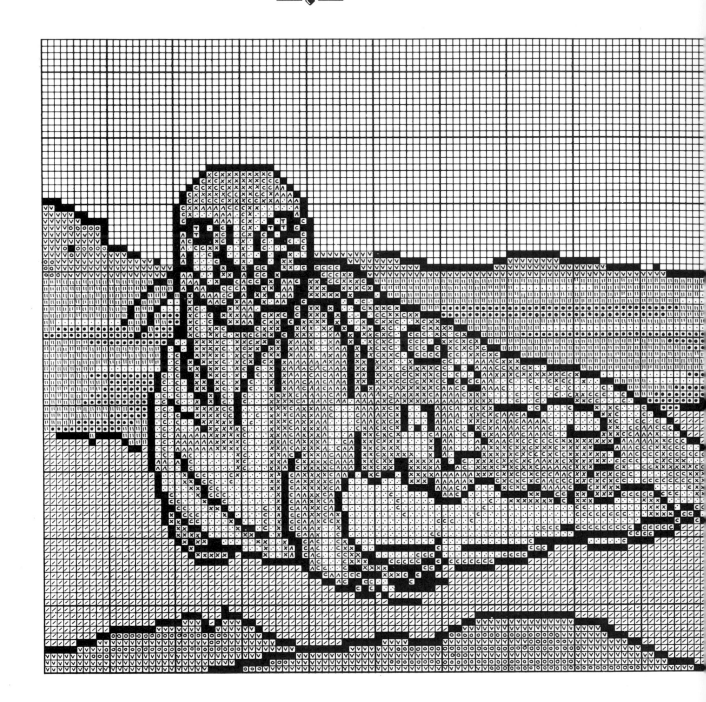

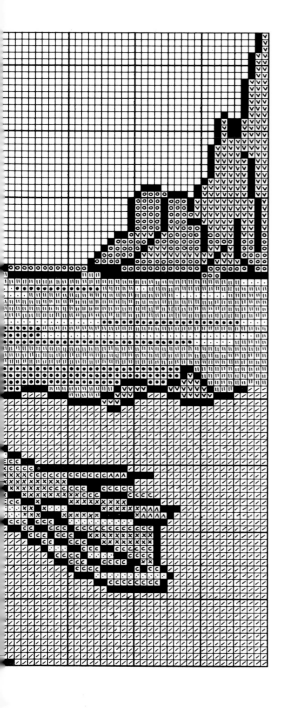

The seal, with its streamlined body and powerful flippers, is especially adapted for life in the water. There are many varieties of seal, living on or near coasts of all the oceans of the world.

The common seal usually inhabits northern harbours, bays and river mouths. It finds movement on land difficult, coming ashore only to sleep, rest and give birth to its young, which are known as pups. Each female bears a single pup. The pup is born on a sandbank or rock, and has to swim as soon as the tide comes in. The seal feeds on fish, squid and other sea creatures, diving to great depths while feeding. Its main predator is the shark.

■	310 black	·	white
V	645 dark beaver grey	⬚	746 off white
O	610 very dark drab brown	T	597 turquoise blue
⊘	3078 very light golden yellow	C	451 shell grey
●	926 medium blue grey	X	3045 dark golden wheat
‖	519 sky blue	∧	648 light beaver grey

Flamingo

◆

The flamingo is a beautiful, colourful bird, most abundant in the tropics of Europe, Asia, Africa and America. It lives in large colonies which can contain more than a million birds. The flamingo nests in shallow ponds, building a mound of mud which dries hard in the sun on which to lay its egg. Each flamingo lays just one white egg, which takes a month to hatch. All the eggs of a colony hatch at roughly the same time. The male flamingo also helps to incubate the eggs. The new-born chick has whitish-grey down with a pink bill and legs. The flamingo chick is strong enough to leave the nest three or four days after hatching.

The flamingo feeds with its head and bill upside-down. As the bird moves forward, it drags its bill in the silt, while the tongue creates a suction, drawing small water plants and animals into the bill. The lower bill remains still, while the upper bill moves slightly, creating a filter.

The flamingo feeds in saline water and because of this, is found only on salt coastal lagoons or in the saline lakes of desert regions. Whenever possible, it will visit fresh water daily to drink and bathe. Its natural food contains a chemical which makes its feathers pink. In captivity, this chemical may be added to its food. There are many types of flamingo, including the greater flamingo, lesser flamingo, Chilean flamingo, Caribbean rosy flamingo and the James flamingo.

Photo on p. 36

■	310 black	●	961 dark dusty rose pink
·	white	⁄	963 very light dusty rose pink
C	794 pale blue	V	472 very light avocado green
L	762 very light pearl grey	Ⅲ	3078 very light golden yellow
Z	414 steel grey	=	726 light topaz yellow
X	471 light avocado green	∧	924 dark blue grey
∴	422 light tan beige	⸤	413 very dark steel grey

FLAMINGO
See pp. 34–5

DOLPHIN
See pp. 38–9

Dolphin

— ◆ —

The bottle-nosed dolphin is the best-known species of dolphin, found mainly in the warm and temperate areas of the Atlantic and Mediterranean. It can grow up to 12 ft (3.6 m) in length and weigh up to 870 lb (394 kg). It swims in a group called a school. It is a slow swimmer, reaching 20 knots only in occasional bursts of speed. It feeds mainly on fish, which it catches and holds in its sharp teeth. The dolphin communicates by producing a wide range of whistles and clicks. It also has a sonar system which can locate objects at a distance.

The bottle-nosed dolphin has a gestation period of 12 to 13 months. The young are born in the summer, and suckled in the way of all mammals. Reaching sexual maturity at about 12 years old, dolphins have been known to live up to 30.

Although in the past many were killed for their oil, adult dolphins have few enemies nowadays.

Photo on p. 37

■	310 black	·.	746 off white
L	415 pale grey	•	white
⧄	414 steel grey	‖	826 medium blue

Beaver

—— ◆ ——

The beaver is the largest water-dwelling rodent of North America. Its coat is fully waterproof with long, coarse, greasy guard hairs lying over the fine dense underfur. Its hind feet are webbed and its front feet are like hands which it uses to carry and handle twigs, branches and mud. It has a long, flattened, scaly tail which it uses as a rudder in the water, or a prop when it sits upright. Its nose and ears close when it is submerged and its eyes are covered by transparent eyelids. It can remain underwater for 15 minutes.

The beaver lives in rivers and lakes and comes ashore to feed on bark from the smaller branches and twigs of willow and aspen. To reach the twigs, however, the beaver often has to fell the entire tree. It is capable of cutting down trees of up to 18 in (45 cm) across with its powerful chisel-like incisor teeth.

The beaver lives underground. If the banks are steep, it will dig a burrow with an entrance beneath the water, but where the banks are low and the water is too shallow, it will build a lodge and dam. Beaver dams are long piles of logs, branches, and stones plastered together with mud. The ponds or small lakes created by these dams are used by the beaver as sites for its dome-shaped lodges.

The fur of the beaver has been sought after by trackers for many centuries, and in many parts of its range it has been exterminated by over-trapping.

■	310 black	⊡	738 very light tan
☒	3078 very light golden yellow	⊤	318 light steel grey
☑	932 light antique blue	⫼	642 dark beige grey
☐	white	◖	413 very dark steel grey
◉	368 light pistachio green	⊙	317 medium steel grey
▤	772 very light loden green	⟦	436 tan brown
∟	3064 spice brown	⊘	319 very dark pistachio green
⋀	838 very dark beige brown		

Hare

◆

The hare is a member of the rabbit family. There are two dozen species of hares, and they are generally distinguished by having longer ears than rabbits and by living in the open rather than in burrows. The young are born well-furred and have their eyes open. They are able to run about almost immediately. The hare is long-legged and high-jumping, speed being its only defence against its predators. Some species can leap 20 ft (6 m) in one bound, and all can change direction between jumps to confuse and try to shake off close pursuers. Hares fight among themselves by biting and kicking with their powerful hind legs.

The European hare lives in the more temperate regions of Europe and Asia, from the British Isles eastward through European Russia. It has also been imported into south-eastern Canada and the north-eastern United States. It is mainly active in the early hours of the morning and the late afternoon, but may also forage for food for a good portion of the night. Its main foods are grass, leaves and bark.

■	310 black	‖	434 light brown
⁄	676 light old gold	∨	3045 dark golden wheat
⊠	610 very dark drab brown	◢	927 blue grey
⊡	white	L	758 pale brick red
⊙	413 very dark steel grey	⋀	318 light steel grey
Z	400 dark mahogany brown	⸱	3022 brown grey
C	976 medium golden brown	⊡	3047 pale golden wheat

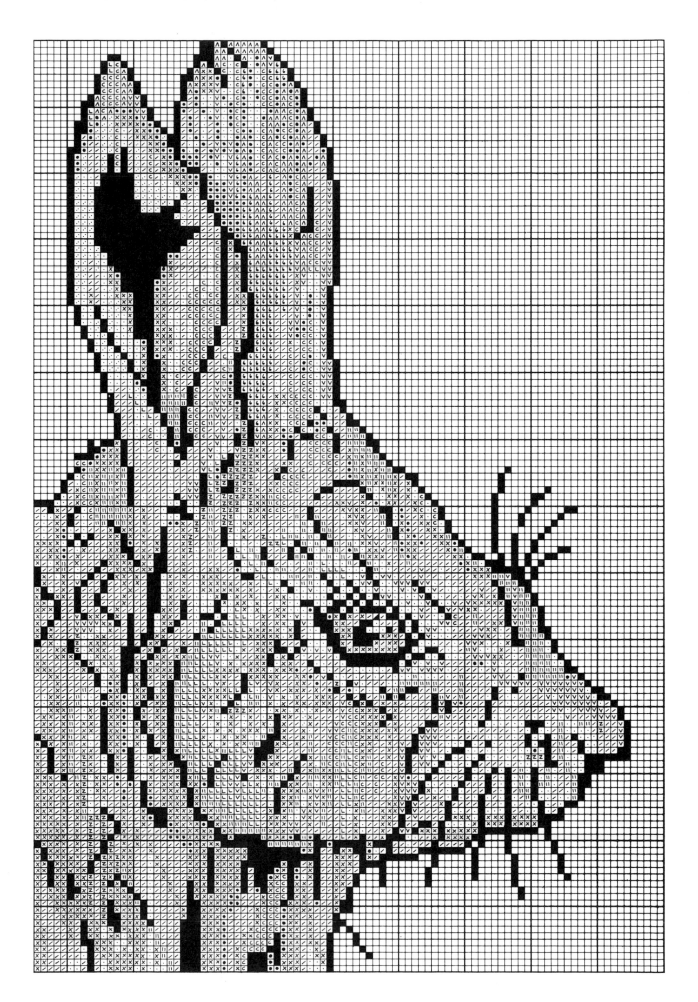

Kangaroo

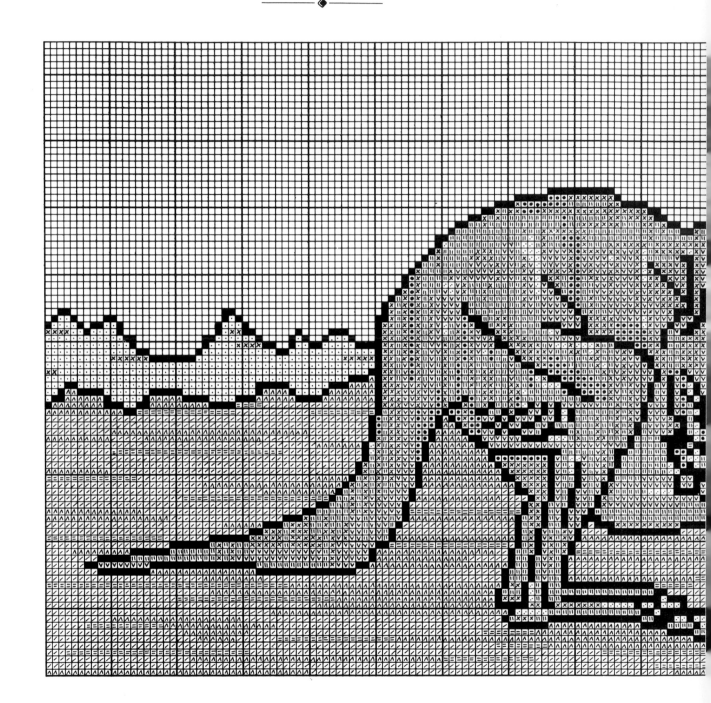

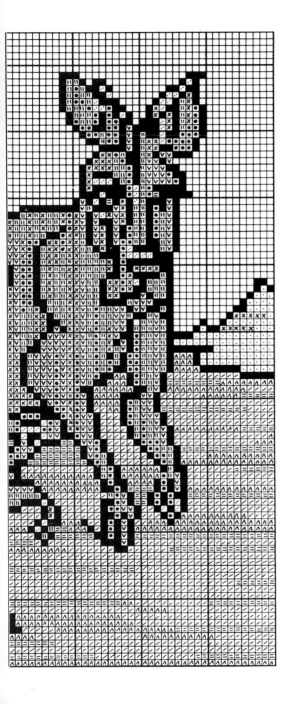

The kangaroo must be the most famous marsupial of Australia and New Guinea. Altogether there are about 50 species of kangaroo, ranging greatly in size. Some are no larger than rats while the great grey kangaroo can grow to over 7 ft (2 m) in length and 200 lb (91 kg) in weight. The kangaroo feeds mainly on grasses and leaves. It has long hind legs and feet which always move in unison, short front legs and feet which can handle food, and a long round tail which acts as a counterbalance, since the kangaroo usually stands upright.

The great grey kangaroo occupies much of Australia's open forest, living in groups called mobs. It can travel at speeds of up to 25 mph (40 kph), with jumps covering a distance of 15 to 20 ft (4.5 to 6 m). Ordinarily, it travels at a more leisurely pace, with jumps of less than 10 ft (3 m).

The kangaroo gives birth to a single baby at a time. The baby is naked when born; it finds its own way to the mother's pouch and develops inside it for a further 26 weeks.

As the forests of Australia were cleared for grazing, the kangaroos increased in number on the new grassland. This resulted in the kangaroos becoming a pest on sheep farms and hundreds of thousands have been killed.

■	310 black	⊟	444 dark lemon yellow
⊠	413 very dark steel grey	⊡	3042 light antique lilac
◫	648 light beaver grey	⋏	422 light tan beige
●	451 shell grey	⧄	3078 very light golden yellow
⋁	437 light tan brown	⊡	762 very light pearl grey

· 45 ·

Stoat

— ◆ —

The stoat is a slender-bodied, short-legged carnivore. The smallest member of the weasel family, it needs little cover to protect it. Where there is suitable food, it occurs in a wide range of habitats from lowland forests to upland moors and even urban areas, hunting by day as well as by night.

The stoat can be found in Great Britain, Ireland and throughout mainland Europe, north of the Alps and the Pyrenees; and also in Asia and most of North America where it is known as the short-tailed weasel. It has a black-tipped tail, and its colouring changes from brown on its back to a creamy white on its underparts. It moults in spring and autumn, and in the colder parts it turns white in winter, although it never loses the black tip to its tail. In Britain an adult male grows to about 12 in (30 cm) plus a $4\frac{1}{2}$ in (11 cm) tail, and weighs up to $11\frac{1}{2}$ oz (320 g). The European mainland, Asiatic and North American stoats are consistently smaller.

The stoat is a solitary creature living in a family group. Its prey consists mainly of small mammals, but it also eats frogs, lizards, small birds, insects and some vegetation. It kills its prey with a powerful bite at the base of the skull.

Unfortunately, the stoat is relentlessly persecuted by man throughout Britain and Europe, and few stoats reach their second birthday.

Photo on p. 48

■	310 black	∧	3362 dark loden green
●	326 very deep rose red	O	869 hazelnut brown
·	white	╱	422 light tan beige
✕	911 medium emerald green	‖	433 medium brown
··	704 bright chartreuse green	∨	3022 brown grey

STOAT
See pp. 46–7

· 48 ·

LEOPARD
See pp. 50–1

Leopard

——— ◆ ———

The leopard, a member of the cat family, can still be found scattered throughout Africa and Asia, although its numbers are dwindling because of man's persecution over the years. Despite their rarity, leopards are still being killed to supply the illegal fur trade.

The leopard is a beautiful creature, renowned for its cunning and savagery. A large male leopard can weigh just under 200 lb (91 kg), the female being considerably smaller. Its prey consists of deer, porcupines, antelopes, monkeys and other small mammals. The leopard is a good climber, and will often wait up in a tree to drop down on its prey. The carcass may then be dragged up into the tree where it cannot be stolen.

Photo on p. 49

- ■ 310 black
- · white
- Ⅲ 703 chartreuse green
- ⦿ 221 very dark mulberry
- ⊠ 415 pale grey
- ⊂ 727 very light topaz yellow
- ⋁ 738 very light tan
- ⧄ 725 topaz yellow

Raccoon

◆

The raccoon, famous for its black 'robber mask' and ringed tail, is a flat-footed mammal familiar in North America, ranging from southern Canada to Panama. It is very active at night, but not wholly nocturnal. The raccoon always lives close to water, as it hunts for most of its food in shallow streams and pools where it finds crayfish, frogs and mussels by feeling in the water with its forepaws. In captivity where it cannot fish, it replaces this activity by washing its food. The raccoon also feeds on insects, wild fruit, corn and small rodents. In most areas, it makes its den in hollow trees.

There are now many urban raccoons inhabiting the lofts and chimney stacks of town and city dwellings, living from dustbins and on scraps that people put out for them.

Most raccoons weigh between 8 and 15 lb (3.6 and 6.8 kg), but some have been known to reach 30 lb (13.6 kg).

Unfortunately, these beautiful and endearing creatures have been trapped for many years to acquire their valuable fur. They are also hunted for sport, usually with dogs. Fully grown raccoons can be dangerous when cornered, and have been known to kill raccoon hounds.

■	310 black	✕	738 very light tan
●	890 very dark evergreen	Ⅲ	436 tan brown
∨	367 dark pistachio green	·	white
∕	704 bright chartreuse green	=	435 very light brown
∧	839 dark beige brown	⊳	433 medium brown
c	413 very dark steel grey	O	453 light shell grey
··	415 pale grey	ε	727 very light topaz yellow
T	318 light steel grey		

Dingo

◆

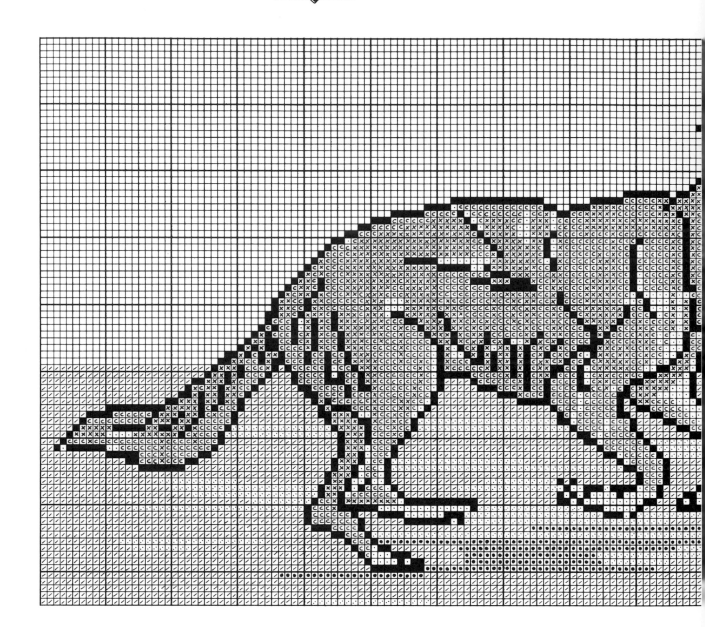

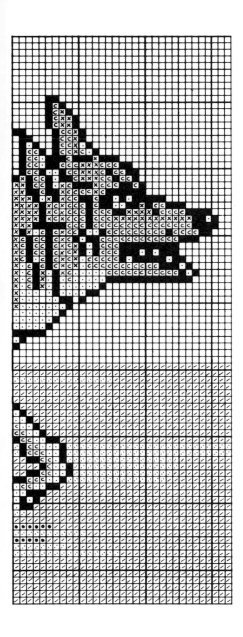

The dingo is the Australian wild dog. It is the only carnivorous non-marsupial mammal native to Australia, having lived there unchanged for at least 8,000 years. It closely resembles the domestic dog, apart from the facts that its pointed, erect ears cannot be laid down and that instead of barking, it yelps and howls mournfully. Legend says that the dingo was once a domestic dog which was carried to Australia thousands of years ago by the aborigines. It grows up to 20 in (50 cm) at shoulder height, weighing up to 44 lb (20 kg). Its coat is mostly reddish-brown with irregular white markings. In captivity, it has been known to live up to 14 years, but in the wild it is widely subject to man's hunting.

The dingo hunts mainly at night, feeding on the native marsupials, rabbits, lizards and grasshoppers. It also sometimes kills domestic sheep and is therefore hunted by sheep-farmers.

Photo on p. 56

■	310 black	⊙	895 very dark green
☒	610 very dark drab brown	⊘	367 dark pistachio green
⊡	white	⊡	906 medium parrot green
⊏	437 light tan brown		

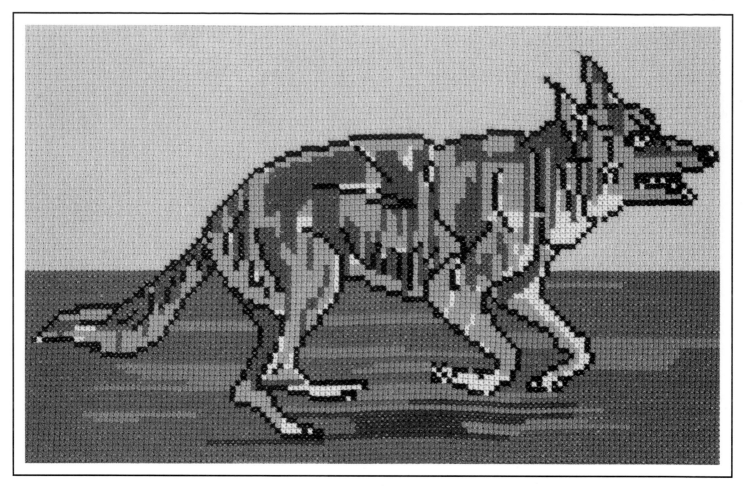

DINGO
See pp. 54–5

TIGER
See pp. 58–9

Tiger

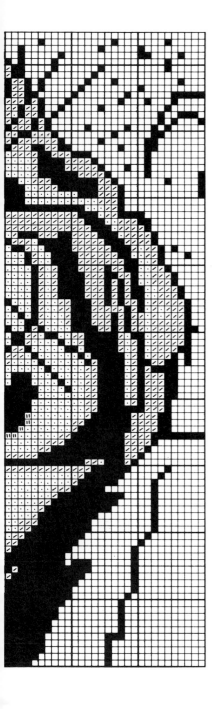

The tiger is the largest of the cat family. It is a beautiful, powerful, striped cat which is widely distributed in Asia, from India to Siberia and Java. The male tiger weighs approximately 500 lb (226 kg) and stands almost 3 ft (0.9 m) high at the shoulder. It leads a solitary life in jungles and grasslands, preferring to be near water. It loves to swim, but is very rarely seen climbing.

The tiger preys on many types of game, ranging from full-grown elephants and bears to crocodiles and fish. It usually hunts alone. The tiger stalks silently, seizing the unwary animal by the throat and frequently breaking its neck on impact. Man-eating tigers are greatly feared, but very rare as the tiger generally avoids humans.

A tigress can give birth to as many as six cubs, but the usual number is three. The cubs usually stay with their mother for a year or more, learning from her the skills of hunting and survival.

Tigers are now becoming rare, partly because their main prey, the blackbuck, is now disappearing. They are also being hunted for their skins to supply the sickening and illegal fur trade.

Photo on p. 57

■	310 black		V	350 light red
·	white		Z	317 medium steel grey
●	221 very dark mulberry		◖	970 light pumpkin orange
⁄	973 bright canary yellow		=	701 dark Kelly green
Ⅲ	971 pumpkin orange		c	677 very light old gold
×	648 light beaver grey			

Panda

—◆—

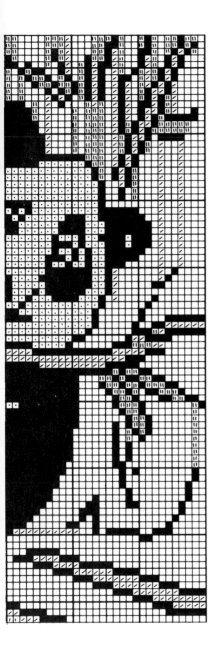

This strange-looking but attractive mammal, which is such a favourite at the zoo, comes from China and Tibet. It is not a true bear, but a member of the raccoon family.

The giant panda can weigh as much as 200 lb (91 kg), and grow up to 6 ft (1.8 m) in length. Largely white in colour, the giant panda has black eyes, ears and legs.

The panda prefers to live on its own, and makes its home in dense bamboo jungles at elevations of up to 14,000 ft (4,260 m) in the remote and inaccessible mountains of southern China and Tibet.

It feeds mainly on bamboo shoots, consuming large amounts per day, which it crushes with its heavy teeth and powerful jaws. It has special pads on its hands to help it hold the bamboo. At one time it was thought that the giant panda ate nothing but bamboo shoots, but it is now known that it also feeds on a variety of other plants, and may eat some meat. Much still remains to be learned about its natural history and habits.

■ 310 black

· white

▥ 703 chartreuse green

◻ 307 lemon yellow

Emperor Penguin

◆

Penguins are flightless, swimming birds of the southern hemisphere. There are about 15 types of penguin. The emperor penguin is the largest member of the family, growing up to 4 ft (1.2 m) in height and weighing up to 75 lb (34 kg). It lives among the ice and snow of the coasts of Antarctica and mates and breeds on the sea ice in the bitter cold and darkness of the Antarctic winter months. The birds live in large colonies, and huddle together for warmth. Each female lays a single egg, and then returns to the sea to feed, leaving the male to incubate the egg alone. It is the only species of penguin which leaves the male to do the incubating. For 64 days he will go without food, while he holds the egg on top of his feet, keeping it off the ice and warm under a loose flap of his skin. When the chick hatches, he is able to feed it on milk that forms in his crop during the long fast. After a few days the female will return from the sea and look after the chick while the male goes off to feed. By the time the chick is ready to go to sea, the milder weather of the Antarctic summer has arrived.

Photo on p. 64

■	310 black	·	white
V	813 light blue	C	352 medium peach
X	977 golden brown	∧	353 peach
Z	762 very light pearl grey	●	413 very dark steel grey
‖	3078 very light golden yellow	⁄	931 antique blue
O	726 light topaz yellow	‹	414 steel grey
4	611 dark drab brown		

EMPEROR PENGUIN
See pp. 62–3

PUFFIN
See pp. 66–7

Puffin

———◆———

The puffin is a member of the auk family, which contains 22 species of seabirds. It spends most of its life at sea, coming ashore only to breed on the cliffs of rocky coasts and islands. It lives in the North Atlantic and breeds around the coasts of Britain. It measures approximately 12 in (30 cm) in length. It is a stocky bird and an excellent swimmer, capable of diving down from the surface of the sea to pursue fish underwater by rowing with its wings and steering with its feet. It can carry about a dozen small fish in its bill.

The puffin's face changes colour with the season. In summer its face is white and its parrot-like bill is bright red and yellow, but in winter its face darkens and the colours of its bill become dull. The bill becomes brighter again in the spring as the breeding season approaches. During the breeding season, facing one another, the puffins do a solemn bill-rapping display which looks most amusing. The puffin is very unusual in that it nests in burrows. It will either use an old rabbit burrow, or use its feet to dig its own short burrow on the cliffs near the sea. It lays a single egg, and once hatched the young puffin is raised in the burrow.

Photo on p. 65

■	310 black	◹	3021 very dark brown grey
·	white	∧	437 light tan brown
V	415 pale grey	∴	827 very light blue
●	347 dark salmon red	=	825 dark blue
X	307 lemon yellow	Ⅲ	3031 very dark brown
Z	807 peacock blue	L	3045 dark golden wheat
C	906 medium parrot green	T	977 golden brown

Badger

◆

The badger is a heavy-bodied, short-legged digging mammal, the most powerful member of the weasel family. It is also the least carnivorous member of the weasel family; the badger eats a wide variety of foods, from burrowing mammals to crawling insects and snails, but it also varies its diet by eating fruit and honey from bees' nests.

The badger is found in Europe, North America and parts of Asia. The badger of Europe and Asia grows to just over 3 ft (0.9 m) in length and is nocturnal, feeding at night on insects, snails, slugs and small mammals, with some vegetable foods. The American badger is similar to that of Europe and Asia, but slightly smaller. It lives on ground squirrels, marmots, prairie dogs and other small rodents, being able to burrow rapidly after prey.

Both European and American badgers inhabit extensive burrows known as setts, which run a long way underground. The sett is a network of tunnels. Deep inside are nests of dead leaves carried in by the badgers.

Unfortunately many badgers lose their lives to the extremely cruel sport of badger baiting in which setts are dug up and terriers sent in to kill the badgers.

■	310 black	⊟	840 beige brown
⧄	white	Ḻ	831 light avocado leaf brown
⊠	702 Kelly green	z	352 medium peach
⋅	3348 light yellow green	y	726 light topaz yellow
⋁	3013 light khaki green	⊞	349 red
‖	413 very dark steel grey	⊡	437 light tan brown
⊙	414 steel grey	⊡	938 dark forest brown
⋀	762 very light pearl grey		

Butterfly

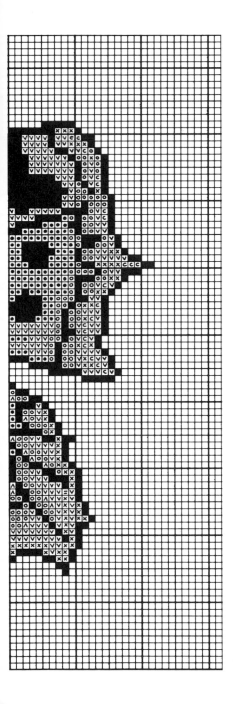

There are more than 100,000 species of butterflies and moths, and these form one of the largest orders of insects, Lepidoptera. Butterflies can be easily distinguished from moths by the fact that they fly by day, as well as having slenderer bodies than moths.

Butterflies undergo metamorphosis before they reach maturity. After mating, the female lays her eggs on the food plant of the caterpillar which will eventually hatch from the egg. The egg will change colour as the caterpillar develops within. When it is ready to hatch the caterpillar eats its way out and starts to feed on the plant.

The caterpillar will spend most of its life feeding and consequently grows very rapidly until it has to shed its skin. It will cast its skin several times, then before becoming a chrysalis or pupa, it will secure itself firmly to a support. It will moult for the last time, and the pupa will emerge. After this, the cells within will break down and the adult butterfly will begin to develop within the pupal shell, emerging when conditions are suitable.

The butterfly then crawls to a suitable site where it rests with its head upwards allowing the wings to open and unfurl to their full size. This will take approximately 15 to 30 minutes, and after allowing the wings to dry and harden, the butterfly is able to fly off in search of food and a suitable mate.

Photo on p. 72

■	310 black	C	632 chocolate brown
●	349 red	O	996 medium electric blue
V	307 lemon yellow	·	318 light steel grey
X	703 chartreuse green	∧	825 dark blue
‖	3363 loden green	=	740 tangerine orange

· 71 ·

BUTTERFLY
See pp. 70–1

SCARLET MACAW
See pp. 74–5

Scarlet Macaw

The macaw is a member of the parrot family. It has a strong, curved, pointed beak with a hinged and movable upper mandible. Each foot has four toes, two turned forwards and two turned backwards, enabling it to perch on one foot while holding its food in the other. It uses both its bill and feet in climbing. The scarlet macaw is native to Central and South America and is one of the largest parrots found there. It often measures 3 ft (91 cm) from its head to the tips of its tail feathers and it is a strong flyer. Its diet consists mainly of fruit, nuts, grain, buds and nectar. Little is known of its breeding habits.

Photo on p. 73

■	310 black	C	996 medium electric blue
●	347 dark salmon red	✕	931 antique blue
Ⅱ	726 light topaz yellow	◪	333 dark lilac
Z	415 pale grey	⋅	745 light yellow
•	white	O	907 light parrot green
V	824 very dark blue	◪	367 dark pistachio green

Koala

———◆———

The koala is native to Australia. It is one of the best-known marsupials, and is often referred to as the 'koala bear', although it is not related to the true bears. The koala weighs less than 30 lb (13.6 kg) and has large tufted ears, wide prominent eyes and short, soft, woolly fur. It lives in the forests of eastern Australia where it spends most of its life up in the trees feeding on the tough, oily leaves of various gum or eucalyptus trees. The oils in the eucalyptus leaves are poisonous to most animals, but the koala's digestive system can cope with them. The koala carries supplies of these leaves to its nest in its cheek-pouches. The young of the koala are carried in the mother's pouch until they are about two months old; later they ride on her back.

The koala is as symbolic of Australia as the kangaroo, but unfortunately many of the eucalyptus forests have been cut down, leaving the koala with fewer places to live. This animal has also been hunted for many years for its fur but is now a protected species.

■	310 black	●	413 very dark steel grey
Z	white	V	300 very dark mahogany brown
+	758 pale brick red	⁄	3031 very dark brown
ᵒ	971 pumpkin orange	L	437 light tan brown
Ⅲ	972 deep canary yellow	·	3047 pale golden wheat
O	973 bright canary yellow	=	648 light beaver grey
∧	700 bright Christmas green	C	436 tan brown
∴	704 bright chartreuse green	⟩	433 medium brown
Ⅲ	471 light avocado green	T	317 medium steel grey
×	730 very dark khaki		

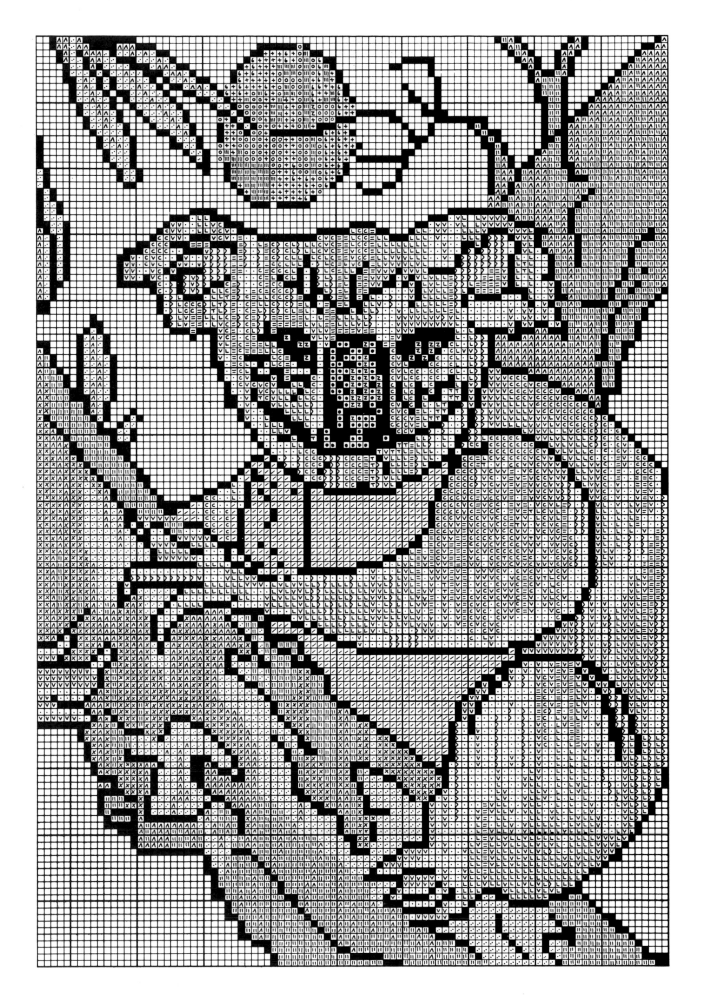

Black Panther

———◆———

The black panther or black leopard is in fact no more than a melanistic variety of the more widespread spotted panther or leopard. It comes from the more heavily forested areas of Asia and Africa. In fact most of the leopards living in primary jungle are of the dark or melanistic form and the black rosettes that form the leopard's characteristic spots are of the same pattern as those on the spotted leopard but can only be seen at close quarters. Cubs of both forms may appear in the same litter, although the black variety is predominant in the humid rain forest of tropical Asia.

■	310 black	y	307 lemon yellow
✗	453 light shell grey	⊘	451 shell grey
·	white	‖	535 dark pewter grey
∧	703 chartreuse green		

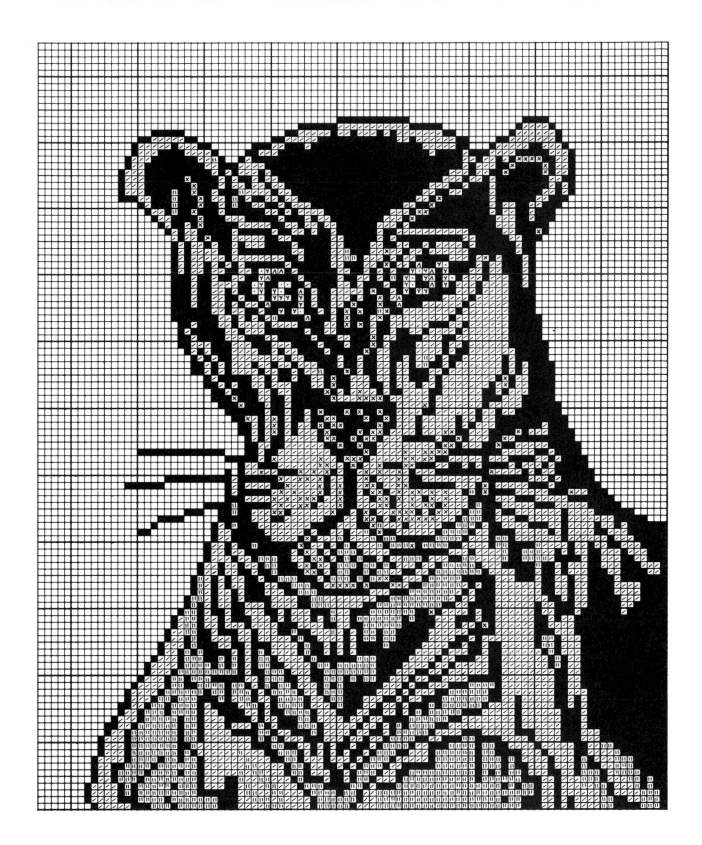

Ibex

— ◆ —

The ibex is the wild goat of Europe, North Africa and parts of Asia. It lives in the mountainous areas of steep cliffs and rocky slopes. It is a very difficult animal to approach, as it startles very easily and panics at the slightest sign of danger. In the Italian Alps, there still survives a protected colony of ibexes. It is believed that our domestic goats may have been derived from the ibex.

The male ibex grows to between 26 and 41 in (65 and 105 cm) in height and weighs between 175 and 220 lb (80 and 100 kg), the female being slightly smaller.

■	310 black	▥	640 very dark beige grey
C	632 chocolate brown	◪	436 tan brown
Z	807 peacock blue	V	3045 dark golden wheat
∧	3346 dark yellow green	⬞	3078 very light golden yellow
X	307 lemon yellow	•	white
▯	739 fawn beige	ɕ	317 medium steel grey
◉	522 drab olive green	=	415 pale grey

Grey Squirrel

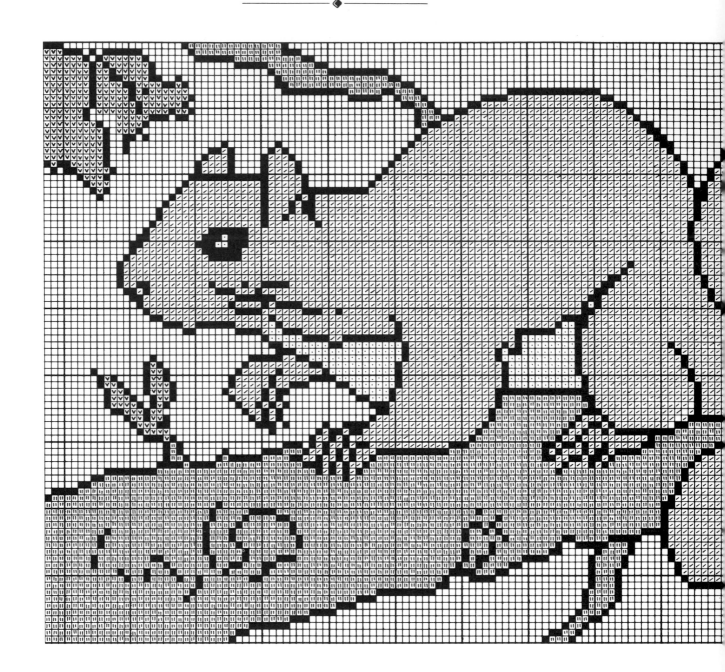

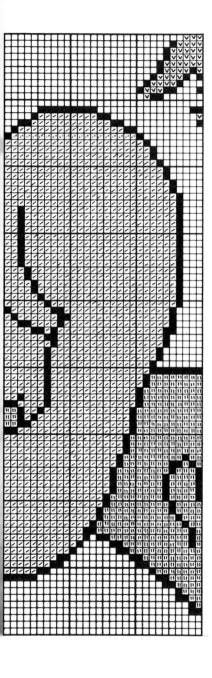

The grey squirrel's original home was in the eastern United States and today its range there runs from the eastern seaboard to the great plains. Between the years 1876 and 1930 it was introduced into Britain and it has spread and multiplied there to such an extent that it is considered a pest and its numbers have to be severely reduced by shooting. It has usurped the habitat of Britain's original red squirrel in many areas.

It lives in forests and feeds on nuts, seeds, fruit and buds. It builds leafy tree nests or dreys, and also nests in holes and hollows in trees. The adult squirrel mates for life. It can have up to two litters in one year, giving birth to an average of four young in each litter. The young leave the nest when they are about six weeks old.

Photo on p. 84

■ 310 black

Ⅲ 801 dark coffee brown

◪ 647 medium beaver grey

· white

∨ 911 medium emerald green

GREY SQUIRREL
See pp. 82–3

RED SQUIRREL
See pp. 86–7

Red Squirrel

———— ◆ ————

The squirrel family is one of the biggest of the rodent groups, containing tree-dwelling squirrels, flying squirrels and ground-dwelling squirrels. Flying squirrels are nocturnal, while the others are active during the day. The wide-eyed, bushy-tailed rodent can be found throughout the world apart from Australia.

The red squirrel is widely distributed in Europe and northern Asia. It thrives best in large mature lowland pine forests, but it has also been found living at heights of up to 6500 ft (2000 m) in the Alps and Pyrenees. It eats mainly pine kernels, acorns, nuts and fungi, but other food is also taken, such as insects and birds' eggs. It detects its food by smell. The red squirrel does not hibernate, and cannot survive for more than a few days without food. When food is plentiful, it will bury it in little stores in the ground, returning later when the supplies are required. Within its home territory, each squirrel will build several dreys, which are round nests made of twigs and lined with moss, grass, shredded bark or pine needles. These are situated in large branch forks and tree trunks.

The red squirrel's greatest enemy is man who has reduced the numbers by the destruction of their habitat. Numbers are also affected by the failure of trees to produce sufficient cones and the many parasites the squirrels carry which can cause disease. In Britain large numbers were recorded at the end of the last century but in the early part of the twentieth century they were reduced by disease at around the same time as the introduction of the grey squirrel which was to take over many of the traditional red squirrel habitats.

Photo on p. 85

■ 310 black		⊡ white	
Ⳑ 3012 medium khaki green		Ⲗ 355 brick red	
⋁ 936 very dark green		⧄ 783 Christmas gold	
⊡ 912 light emerald green		◉ 898 very dark coffee brown	

Brown Bear Cub

◆

The brown bear is the biggest land carnivore, having had no serious predator until the coming of man. It used to be widespread in woodlands with good undergrowth across Europe, Asia and North America. In Europe today, however, it has been reduced to a fraction of its previous abundance, having been driven back into remote mountainous areas of northern Spain, the Pyrenees, Germany, Poland and the Balkans, and remaining common only in Russia and Scandinavia. Because of its size, the brown bear is relatively slow-moving, making active hunting difficult. Because of this, it has become mainly herbivorous, although it will take anything edible such as small mammals, ground-nesting birds, fishes and insects. Although the brown bear does not hibernate in the strict sense, an abundance of autumn food allows it to build up a layer of fat which enables the bear to remain inactive through much of the winter.

Man has reduced the bear's numbers dramatically over the years by destroying its habitat and hunting it for its fur, fat, teeth and claws. It was also killed for sport. It is now an endangered species, and hunting it for sport is forbidden in some countries.

■	310 black	z	white
x	3012 medium khaki green	⦀	809 delft blue
⧄	746 off white	F	309 deep rose red
c	913 medium nile green	∧	561 dark aqua blue green
v	839 dark beige brown	●	895 very dark green
‖	436 tan brown	∴	704 bright chartreuse green
·	738 very light tan	⊓	644 medium beige grey

Toco Toucan

———◆———

The toucan is a beautiful, brightly coloured bird which lives in the jungle treetops in Central and South America. It does not sing, but it makes a loud, harsh, croaking sound which can carry for a distance of half a mile through the jungle. Its brightly coloured bill is hollow, but braced inside with spongy tissue for strength and lightness. It has a long, hard narrow tongue which helps it pick fruit off the trees. The coloured bill may help birds of the same species recognize each other, and is useful for reaching, plucking and crushing its food before swallowing. The toucan nests in hollow trees, laying two to four white eggs. The female toucan will poke her bill out of the nesting hole to frighten off predators. The toucan also sleeps in tree cavities with its bill held over the centre of its back, and its tail tilted forward to cover it.

Photo on p. 92

■	310 black	‹	312 light navy blue
Ⅱ	3051 dark grey green	z	518 light Wedgwood blue
O	701 dark Kelly green	∴	744 medium yellow
L	704 bright chartreuse green	c	415 pale grey
◹	413 very dark steel grey	·	white
7	317 medium steel grey	V	741 medium tangerine orange
◉	930 dark antique blue	X	720 dark orange

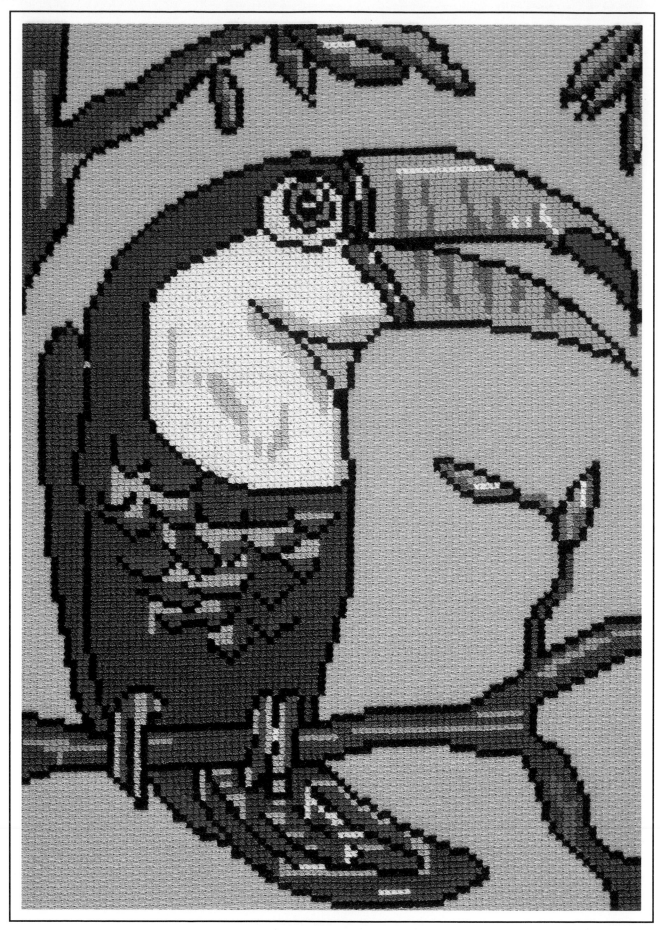

TOCO TOUCAN
See pp. 90–1

RED DEER
See pp. 94–5

Red Deer

◆

The red deer is the largest truly wild animal to be found over most of central and western Europe. It weighs from 200 lb (91 kg) to more than 500 lb (226 kg). The male deer is known as a stag, and the female, a hind. Originally, the red deer could be found throughout Europe, western Russia and northern Africa. But after being hunted for hundreds of years, it has been eradicated in many areas. According to legend only noblemen were privileged to hunt these deer. Specially trained breeds of dog known as stag-hounds were used in the chase.

In Britain, the red deer is thought of as a highland species, as herds continue to survive on Exmoor and on the Scottish hills. In the rich lowland forests of eastern Europe, however, the deer grow to a far larger size. The size of their territory varies according to the habitat and can be almost 2000 acres (800 hectares) for a highland stag. Herd size also varies with habitat, while diet ranges from tree bark and shoots to grasses and farm crops.

The red deer is at its most prominent in October, when the stag enters the hind herds and heralds his readiness to mate by giving a loud moaning bellow which rings through the hills and woods, attracting females but warning off rivals.

Photo on p. 93

■	310 black	▨	918 very dark copper
Ⅲ	3011 dark khaki green	Z	3022 brown grey
⫶	3013 light khaki green	⊞	758 pale brick red
C	470 medium avocado green	⊡	413 very dark steel grey
V	437 light tan brown	∧	801 dark coffee brown
·	white	O	436 tan brown

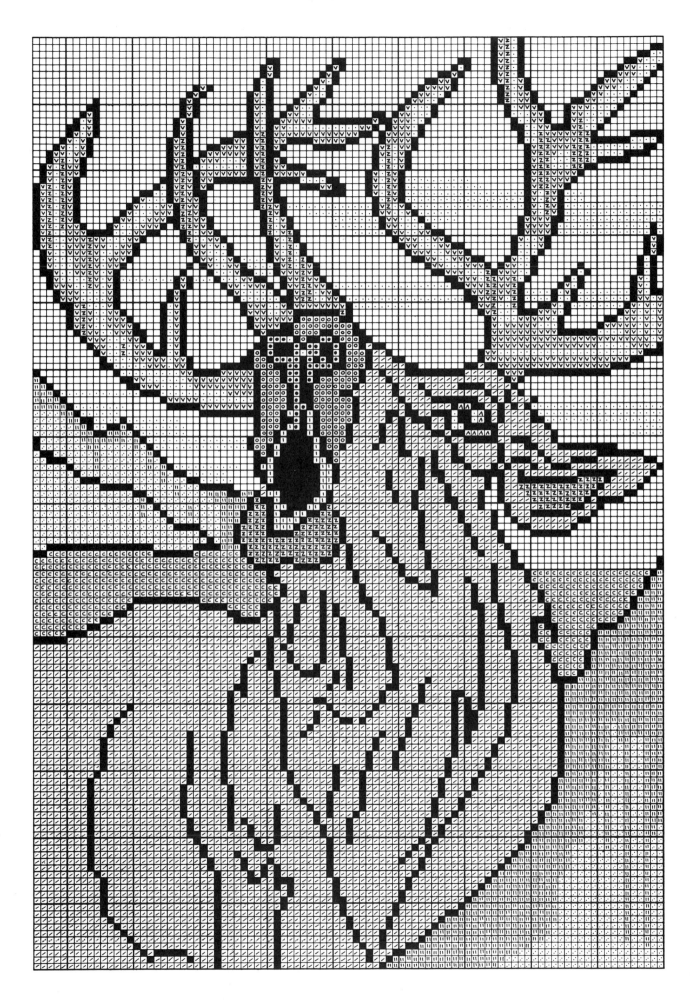

Dormouse

———◆———

There are several types of dormouse living in Europe, Asia and Africa, but the best-known is the European dormouse, found from the Atlantic Ocean eastward across Europe into Russia. The European dormouse was introduced into England around 1890, and has become well established in many localities.

The body of the dormouse measures around $1\frac{1}{2}$ in (3.8 cm) in length, and it has a long, bushy tail. It has soft, fluffy fur, and is rather like a small squirrel in appearance. It feeds mainly on nuts and fruit, and will often climb trees to obtain its food. It puts on extra fat before its winter hibernation, and makes its nest in hollow trees, tree stumps or piles of dead leaves.

■	310 black	⊘	729 medium old gold
⊠	3363 loden green	⊡	676 light old gold
⊻	704 bright chartreuse green	⋀	831 light avocado leaf brown
‖	702 Kelly green	⊟	921 copper
·	white	⬤	321 Christmas red

Harvest Mouse

The harvest mouse is the smallest of the European rodents, its overall length being around $5\frac{1}{2}$ in (14 cm), half of this being accounted for by its slender tail. It can be found through most of Europe with the exception of Ireland, Scandinavia, the far north and most of Spain, Italy and Greece. It also extends eastwards through much of Asia to Japan.

The harvest mouse is mainly nocturnal, but can be found during the daytime searching for the seeds, fruits and insects on which it feeds. Modern agricultural methods have expelled it from its traditional home in the grain fields, but it survives in meadows and waste ground. The breeding season starts in late spring, when the female builds her nursery nest from leaves which are still attached to living plants, in cereal crops or coarse grasses. Up to seven blind and helpless young are born. They develop very quickly and the mother will drive them away from the nest when they are 16 days old to allow time for the production of a second litter. The lifespan of a harvest mouse in the wild is very short: usually between 6 and 18 months, since its predators include both mammals and birds.

■	310 black	T	725 topaz yellow
V	321 Christmas red	●	680 dark old gold
X	911 medium emerald green	‖	729 medium old gold
Z	954 nile green	•	white
·	3348 light yellow green	c	676 light old gold
∧	320 medium pistachio green	╱	677 very light old gold
C	677 very light old gold	═	738 very light tan

Otter

◆

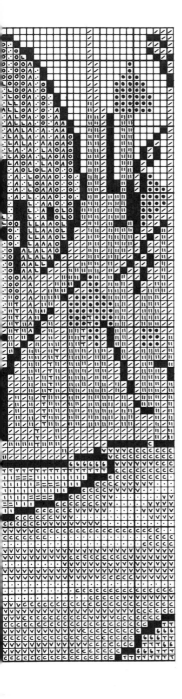

There are about 17 species of otter found in rivers and lakes around the world, and it is one of the largest members of the weasel family. The male otter is called a dog and can measure up to 45 in (115 cm) in length, including its tail, and weigh up to 33 lb (15 kg). The female is called a bitch and is much smaller, often weighing no more than 22 lb (10 kg). The otter is ideally adapted for life in the water, with its streamlined body, small ears, long powerful tapering rudder-like tail and webbed feet which enable it to swim with grace and agility, reaching speeds of up to $7\frac{1}{2}$ mph (12 kph). Its large lungs allow it to dive and stay underwater for up to four minutes, during which time it can chase fish and dig for small animals in the river bed. Its coat consists of a dense undercoat of fine hairs which trap a blanket of air around the body and, over this, long guard hairs which clamp down to waterproof it. This, plus a layer of fat beneath the skin, keeps the animal warm despite the cold water. The otter does not hibernate, but it is less active in the winter, spending most of its time in its underground den or holt feeding mainly on amphibians, crayfish and other cold-blooded animals. During warmer weather, although it prefers fish, the otter will also feed on snails, water voles and young birds. It may produce cubs at any time of the year, but a litter consisting of two or three young is normally born in the early summer.

■	310 black	⊟	3052 medium grey green
●	444 dark lemon yellow	V	519 sky blue
‖	703 chartreuse green	C	807 peacock blue
⁄	436 tan brown	·	white
T	632 chocolate brown	∧	451 shell grey
Z	699 Christmas green	O	3022 brown grey
‹	644 medium beige grey	∴	3032 medium beige
⊞	762 very light pearl grey	L	3033 very light beige

Wolf

The wolf is a member of the dog family, and is thought to be the ancestor of the domestic dog. Once common over most of North America, Europe and Asia, it has been persecuted so extensively by man that it is now extinct over much of this area. In places where it has not entirely died out, it exists only in very small numbers. In fact, man has continually pushed the grey wolf further into the wilderness. It is now common only in North America, Canada and Alaska.

Many wolves live in groups called packs, hunting within a scent-marked territory. The foundation of the pack is a mother and her cubs. When the cubs grow up, they continue to hunt together under her leadership. Other wolves live alone or in pairs, often joining the pack for winter. A pack usually consists of no more than ten wolves.

The wolf's main prey is deer, although it will also steal domestic sheep and cattle when it gets the chance. If hungry, it will also feed on mice, frogs and even roots and berries. The wolf is a very strong runner and chases its prey until it can snap and tear at it, usually foraging at night.

Photo on p. 104

- ■ 310 black
- ⊡ white
- △ 725 topaz yellow
- 7 498 dark Christmas red
- ▽ 3325 baby blue
- ◪ 415 pale grey
- ‖ 680 dark old gold
- ● 3031 very dark brown
- ⊠ 414 steel grey

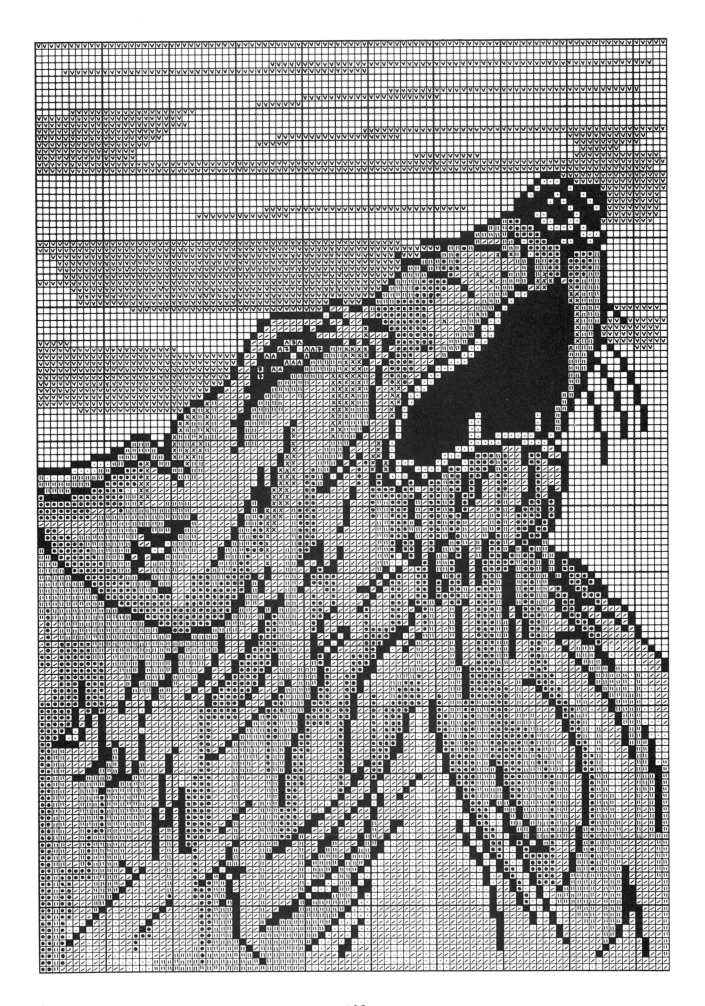

WOLF
See pp. 102–3

BALD EAGLE
See pp. 106–7

Bald Eagle

◆

The bald eagle is the national bird of the United States of America, and is pictured on the Great Seal. Also found in Canada, it is slightly larger than the golden eagle, and is not in fact bald, despite its name, but has a head of white feathers. Its favourite food is fish which it often obtains by perching to watch another bird of prey, the osprey, fish, waiting for it to drop its catch, and then swooping down to steal it. So fast is the bald eagle in flight, that it has the fish firmly in its talons long before it hits the ground or water below. The bird is best known for its powerful flight and keen eyesight.

Photo on p. 105

■	310 black	◉	3031 very dark brown
⧄	931 antique blue	·	white
✕	3325 baby blue	⌵	3023 light brown grey
⫴	729 medium old gold	Z	726 light topaz yellow
C	420 dark hazelnut brown	⫼	3078 very light golden yellow

Giraffe

◆

The giraffe is the world's tallest mammal, with the male having been known to stand more than 18 ft (5.5 m) high. It is a social animal, living in a herd commanded by bulls on the African plains. It feeds mainly on leaves and branches, plucking the leaves with its lips and long (up to 18 in or 45 cm) sensitive tongue. The giraffe can go without drinking for quite long periods of time. When it does stop for water it drinks by spreading its legs wide apart and bending them slightly, enabling its long neck to reach the water.

When it runs the giraffe looks most peculiar, since it moves front and hind legs on the same side simultaneously. It is a gentle animal but is quite capable of giving a nasty kick. It is usually silent, since its vocal cords are degenerate, but it can moo or grunt weakly. There are several varieties of giraffe, distinguished by differences in coat patterns and by the number of horns on the top of their skulls. Both the male and female giraffe have horns or bony knobs on the top of the skull which are covered with skin and tufts of hair.

■	310 black	Z	white
Ⅲ	3045 dark golden wheat	∕	3348 light yellow green
·	3078 very light golden yellow	V	911 medium emerald green
X	632 chocolate brown	L	307 lemon yellow
T	597 turquoise blue		

Zebra

◆

The zebra is the small black-and-white striped horse of Africa. Species include Grevy's zebra, Grant's zebra, the mountain zebra and Chapman's zebra. The zebra lives on open grasslands in large herds which often contain a thousand or more animals. The female zebra, known as the mare, will usually bear just one foal, which is up and about within an hour of birth. It will begin to graze within a few weeks, but is generally not weaned for 8 to 13 months. Although they can breed annually, most mares miss a year owing to the strain of rearing a foal.

■	310 black
☒	807 peacock blue
⊡	white
☑	3022 brown grey
◪	676 light old gold

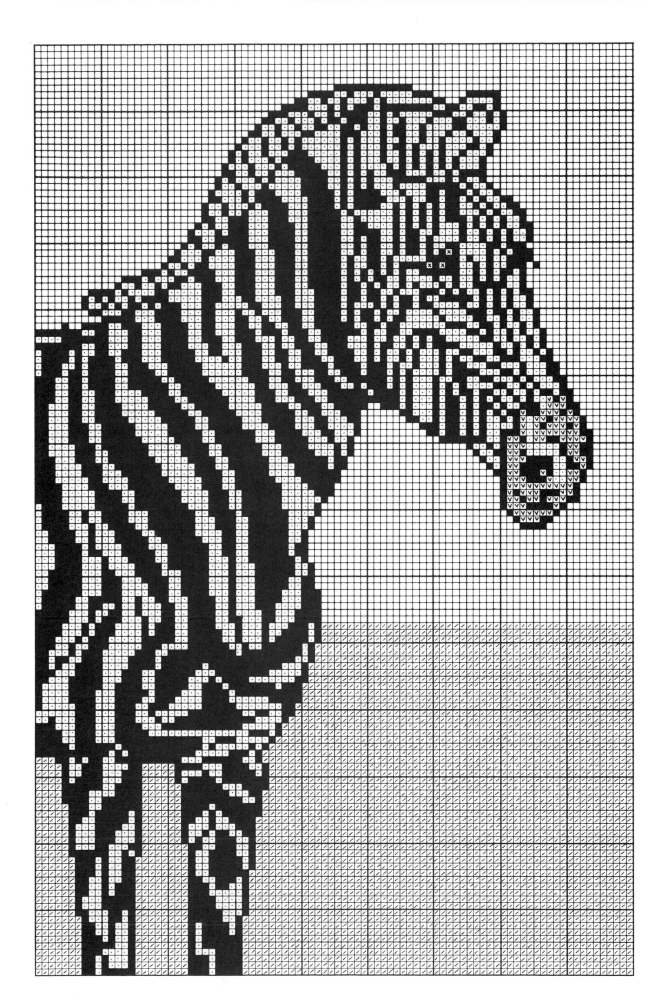